Brock Bottoms

Brock Bottoms, set in the idyllic wooded valley of the River Brock, is a well known and much frequented beauty spot. However, few people realize that beneath the tangled undergrowth lie the remains of an industrial community. It is hard to believe that it is barely forty years since the last inhabitant left the valley, so effectively have the ravages of time worn away the traces of the settlement. By taking the footpath alongside the river towards Bannister Hey, it is still just possible to find the ruins. Wyre Borough Council has recently fenced the mill building for safety reasons and their permission is required in order to gain full access. Nevertheless, enough is visible over the fence to give an adequate impression of the site.

The Brock Bottoms community in 1912, showing the mill on the right with the tall chimney and Bottom Row cottages on the left.

The present remaining wall of the mill. The mill building itself had been badly damaged by fire around 1860 and maps show a change in the building plan after this date. The lower part of the building shown here may be a survival from the earlier construction.

Brief history of the mill

It is not known exactly who was responsible for building the settlement, but it is probable that at the beginning of the 1790s a Preston firm, Lorimer and Company, built a cotton spinning factory at Brock Bottoms. In the early years of industrialization mills were dependent on water power for their operation, which meant that the first cotton factories were erected beside rivers, often in places without previous settlement. Such was the case of Brock Bottoms and twenty cottages were built near the mill to accommodate the work-force, and a small industrial community was formed.

The mill at Brock Bottoms had a chequered history. For more than half its life it was a cotton spinning factory, and certainly in its early years it proved to be a prosperous concern, judging from an advertisement for the sale of Lorimer's shares in the mill in 1796. This describes the mill as having

> new and complete mill gear, and 16 good spinning frames, proper and sufficient to supply 1152 spindles, all new and in good condition, and a

Brock Bottoms

A History of the Mill and the Community

by

S. Parker

Lancashire County Books, 1992

Acknowledgements

I am grateful to Mr P. J. Taylor and Mr C. Aspin for providing information used in this book. I would also like to thank Ms Tamara Gabrysch for the excellent diagram of the watermill, and Mrs E. Foley, Mr T. Farrell (formerly of the *Lancashire Evening Post*) and the many other people too numerous to mention who offered their valuable assistance.

This book is dedicated to
my dear wife Emily and my son Sidney

Brock Bottoms
A History of the Mill and the Community

by S. Parker

First edition, November 1992
Published by Lancashire County Books, 143 Corporation Street, Preston
Designed and typeset by Carnegie Publishing Ltd., 18 Maynard Street, Preston
Printed and bound in the UK by T. Snape & Co., Preston

ISBN 1-871236-18-5

joiner's and smith's shop with hearths, fluting engine, benches and all sorts of tools and implements suitable to the business, together with a warehouse, 20 cottages and a stable, the whole lately erected at an expense of near £4000 and now advantageously carrying on by the surviving partners.

At this period it appears that Brock Bottoms was a thriving community but it was not to last. Even by 1807 there is evidence that all was not well at the mill, for in that year an advertisement appeared in the Blackburn Mail for the sale of the mill and cottages, the owner John Eamer having gone bankrupt.

Little is known about the Brock Bottoms mill from this time until Richard Kenyon took control of it around 1829, at first in partnership with a man called Kilshaw, but from approximately 1832 until 1850 as sole owner. For much of this period the mill was struggling to survive. Kenyon was declared bankrupt in May 1837 but was solvent again by the end of the year. However, the mill itself was still having difficulties, with conditions deteriorating still further in the next decade. The censuses of 1841 and 1851 show the Brock Bottoms community in a state of decay with houses uninhabited and several of the remaining occupants in receipt of poor-relief. Around 1852 the firm of Burton and Whitehead took over the mill, but it would never regain the prosperity of its early years. A fire sometime around 1860, when under the ownership of an unknown co-operative, sounded the death knell for the mill as a cotton

The Mill and Bottom Row Cottages in 1905.

spinning factory.

Although the mill at Brock Bottoms was probably one of the first water-powered spinning factories to be established in the Fylde area, it was destined never to prosper. It was far too small and isolated to be able to compete against the large steam-powered factories which were developing rapidly in the nearby towns of Preston and Blackburn.

The site was not abandoned, however, but rebuilt by two brothers, Richard and William Bond, in about 1861 and converted into a roller-making factory, rollers being parts used in spinning factories. The mill was still a very small concern employing only ten men, but it must have encountered some success for it survived over twenty years, though not under the same ownership. It is not known why the roller-making factory ceased production, but around 1891 the mill underwent yet another change of use; this time it was converted by P. J. B. Parker into a file-making factory. It was used for this purpose until 1936 when it finally closed, its last owner being Crompton Crompton from Leyland. For some time after, the mill was open as a cafe on the ground floor, whilst the top floor was used for dancing on Saturday nights, with the Calder Vale Band as the resident musicians.

The decline of the mill at Brock Bottoms is hardly surprising given its isolation and limited production capacity. What is surprising is that it lasted so long. In spite, or maybe because of its successive changes in ownership and use, it was still able to maintain production into the 1930s, which in itself is a remarkable achievement.

Crompton Crompton and his wife, Eleanor, who came from Leyland to take over the mill in the early 20th century. They are pictured here in their 1902 Darracq, which frequently had to be towed up Bannister Hey by two work-horses because the engine was not sufficiently powerful.

The watermill

The mill at Brock Bottoms was originally a watermill, and water continued to be the source of power until the early twentieth century. By the 1840s two reservoirs were in use. These were fed by a mill race from a pond of water held back by a weir in the river a short distance upstream. The water from the mill race supplied the upper reservoir, also known as the lodge, which in turn fed the lower reservoir, thus powering an overshot waterwheel housed within the factory buildings. In an overshot waterwheel the water was directed over the top of the wheel, filling buckets on the far side whose weight caused it to turn. A tailrace then returned the water to the river.

The era of the watermill ended in the 1930s when the weir, which was 41 feet long and 6 feet high, was damaged by floods. £200 was spent on a replacement but the new weir leaked and the constructor who had built it had gone bankrupt. A gas engine was installed to replace the waterwheel, but the money lost on the new weir eventually pushed the Cromptons into closing the business.

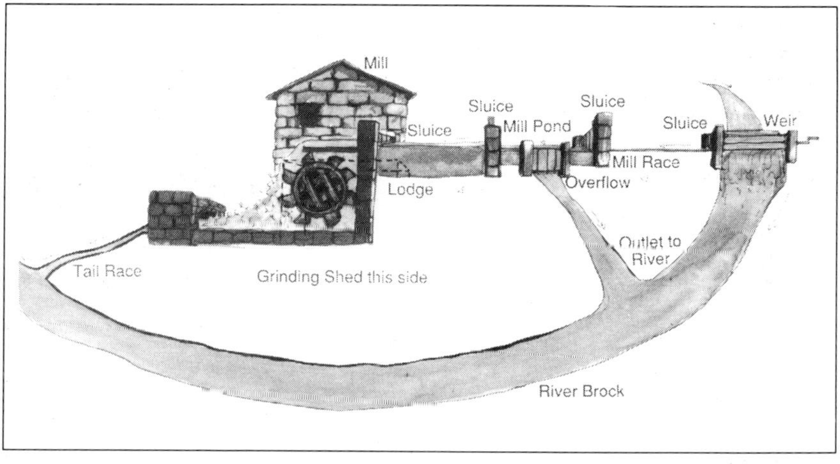

Artist's impression of the layout of Brock Bottoms watermill.

Right: *the weir before it was damaged by floods in the 1930s.*
Below: *the remains of the weir today.*

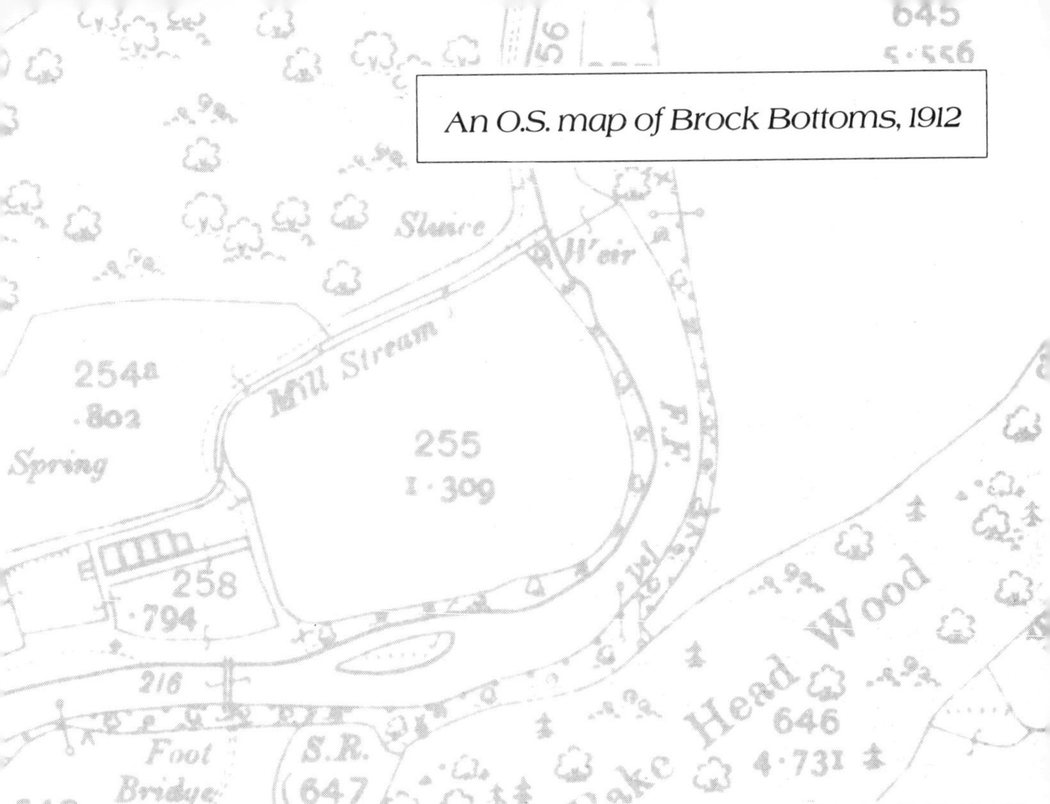

An O.S. map of Brock Bottoms, 1912

***Above**: the mill lodge in 1936.*
***Left**: the lodge as it is today, hidden by the undergrowth.*

The file-making factory and its remains

In the early twentieth century, when the mill came into the ownership of Crompton Crompton, the waterwheel was still in use and remained so for some time, but trouble with the weir caused the wheel to work inefficiently and so a Crossley Gas Engine was installed. The gas engine, like the water wheel before it, powered the bellows for the mill forge as well as turning the grinding wheels used for work on the files. Old worn out files were sent to the mill from Midland Rail, Leyland Motors and also from the local farmers to be remade into new ones.

The files were melted down individually, in a coke furnace kept alight by the bellows, then manually hammered out into shape on stone slabs to a size of 12" x 1½". They were then resurfaced on the grindstones in the grinding shed and finally annealed to give them a 'brand-new' appearance.

Local farmers would use these files for sharpening their mowing machines and scythes. The cost to recondition the files in 1905 would have been 4d each.

Two horses and carts were used to transport the newly surfaced files from the mill to Brock Station where they would be delivered to Leyland Motors and Midland Rail by train.

The remains of the wheelhouse.

Stone slabs, on which files were hammered flat.

Old grindstones on which the metal files would have been resurfaced.

The original inhabitants of Brock Bottoms worked in the mill, indeed the houses were built for the work-force as has already been noted. Over the decades, with the changing fortunes of the mill, the community became more diverse and agricultural labourers from the local farms (as well as the factory workers) rented the cottages. In fact, the settlement continued to be inhabited long after the mill ceased to operate.

The houses in Brock Bottoms were built in two rows, Bottom Row adjacent to the mill and opposite the lodge bank, and Top Row, as the name would suggest, on higher ground further upstream. Although there were initially twenty cottages the number inhabited dwindled over the years

Bottom Row cottages during the heavy snows of 1913.

Top Row with the wash-house on the right-hand end, built from the ruins of those cottages destroyed by fire. This photograph of 1945 is one of the last to be taken whilst Brock Bottoms was still inhabited. Both rows of cottages were condemned in 1945 and the last residents left in 1951.

Ruins of Top Row just visible above the undergrowth.

Bottom Row in 1910.

The remains of a stone wall are all that are left of Bottom Row today.

Top Row cottages after their destruction by fire in 1899. Only four of the original eight cottages survived.

through a process of general decay and destruction by fire so that only eight cottages survived to 1951, when the last inhabitant left the valley. The cottages were constructed of stone; the dressed stone at the windows and doors came from the Delph Quarry at Claughton whilst the rest was random stone taken from the river. The typical lay-out of these cottages was in the two-up, two-down style consisting of a front-room, back kitchen and two bedrooms above with a dividing partition. The rooms were small by today's standards, the front-room measuring about fourteen by eight feet and the cramped kitchen only fourteen by four feet. Overcrowding must have been a severe problem when one considers the large families of the nineteenth century. Nine, ten and even eleven people are recorded as living in a single cottage in Brock Bottoms.

Living conditions would have changed very little over the years for there was never any piped water or electricity in Brock Bottoms, indeed modern life had largely passed it by. Water was obtained from the river itself, although some residents collected rainwater in tanks. Bathing and washing must have been arduous tasks. A wash-house was built after 1912 at the end of the Top Row with stone left over from fire damaged cottages. This was for the general use of the community and contained a boiler, dolly tub, posser and mangle. However, washing was still taken down to the river to be rinsed, even in the 1940s.

The plentiful supply of logs from the woods provided fuel for heating and cooking, and some coal was used, though this was more difficult to acquire given the isolation of the community. The nearest shop was a long walk over the fields at Brock station, so the inhabitants of Brock Bottoms relied on their own garden plots for much of their food, whilst the local farmers also supplied them.

There can be little doubt that living conditions in Brock Bottoms were austere but the beautiful setting and clean country air acted as some compensation for the hardships. Certainly in the nineteenth century the inhabitants of Brock Bottoms would have had a better quality of life than their counterparts in the overcrowded, unhealthy industrial towns, although they were probably as poverty-stricken. Even in the 1930s wages at the mill were extremely low: a foreman received £1 and a labourer only 15 shillings for a fifty-four hour week, compared with the average textile wage of £1 14s. 6d., a spinner earning upwards of £3 for a forty-eight hour week.

Brock Bottoms was never a prosperous community, but the fact that it survived into the mid-twentieth century, even beyond the closure of the mill, is an indication of the charm of the area. Brock Bottoms still holds a great attraction for people, and who would not dream of living in such an idyllic spot, even today?

On the right, Mr. J. Potter, the last employee to work in the mill, with myself on the left, one of the last residents to live in the Top Row cottages.